Business Management

Football Style

By Glen Lucky Drake

Table of Contents

Suggested Reads and Training:
One Minute Manager by Ken Blanchard (all of his books)
Major Account Sales Strategy by Neil Rackham
Competitive Strategy by Michael E. Porter
Mike Holt Enterprises, Electrical Training Programs
Disney Leadership Program

Chapter 1

Intro

Let me start by saying that you don't have to understand football or be a fan to get the principles taught in this lesson. The analogies used are very basic to the game and will be easy to follow even if you never followed the game.

When I am asked the question, "How would you explain your management style?" I respond with "Football Management". Football Management? What is that? Oh, if I only had a dime... Over the years I have read several books on management, and how to manage people. There are many books that have solid, well rounded, ideas on how to effectively get what you need out of your employees. But it always seems that most people lose something in translation or implementation. I spent many years playing football as a youth, and played for many talented teams. I learned at a very young age what it meant to be a member of a team, how to motivate a team, and how to get repeatable results from a team. It is those lessons that I took with me into my adulthood and used to become a highly effective manager. In the following pages you will see how Football Management works, and why it has been so effective for me throughout my career. This style will transcend most every discipline due to the principles of human nature.

Chapter 2

It All Starts with the Team

What makes a team?

The technical definition of a team is, a group of people involved in the same activity, with a common goal. The ironic part of this definition is that in business, the Goal is what most people are confused about. Really? How can a team that has been put together by a company not know what the goal is? We will cover more on this later.

I will go a little further and say that a team needs to clearly understand the following:

1. What is our goal?

2. What is my role?

3. How will I know how I am doing?

So, my definition of a successful team would be: a group of people involved in the same activity, with a common goal, fully understanding their role, the expectations for the team, and how they will be measured and rewarded. Sounds simple right? Well, it should be, but it never seems to work out that way.

Hopefully you are starting to see what I am talking about with the Football analogy. Imagine a Football Team who didn't know:

☐ What's the object of the game? (Scoring, crossing the goal line, kicking a field goal.)

☐ What position they played. (Quarterback, Receiver, Linebacker, offense or defense)

☐ What a first down is, or a penalty. (Measurable successes, or failures)

How successful do you think this team would be? You could literally put a team of all-stars together and still never score a single point.

To put together a winning team in business or anywhere you need to follow this basic outline:

☐ Make sure that your team knows what the objective is.

☐ Make sure your team knows what their role is within the team.

☐ Makes sure your team knows what is expected of them.

☐ Make sure your team knows how they will be measured and what their reward will be.

☐ Make sure your team is driven.

☐ Make sure your team has the requirements of a high performing team.

☐ Make sure you coach them properly.

☐ Make sure you constantly evaluate and adjust where needed.

Chapter 3

What Drives a Team?

I have covered that a team cannot come together without a common goal, clearly defined roles, and a measurable performance guide to know how they are doing. However, that is not enough to motivate a team. While the above outlines the structure, there is an emotional aspect to the team as well. The key emotional aspects are:

☐ A sense of purpose

☐ Support

☐ Comradery

☐ Success

Purpose. If you put together the most talented people in any given field and supply them with all the structure mentioned thus far, the chances of them being successful are limited. The reason being, they lack a sense of purpose. Yes, they do have a common goal, but just a common goal is not a sense of purpose. Human nature dictates that we need to know we are making a difference on some level, or the team will eventually run out of steam. For instance, take a football team and remove the scoreboard. While the team shares the common goal, to cross the goal line, there is no purpose if you don't score. Eventually after the team moves up and down the field, crossing the goal line many times, they will start to lose interest and wonder; why are we doing this? That is why you need a sense of purpose in business. While your team may all know what the common goal is, they may not feel a sense of purpose. This sense of purpose needs to be renewed constantly with the team. They need reaffirmation of why they are doing what they do and the difference they are making. This will keep their sense of purpose charged in their mind and keep them motivated to stay on task.

Support. Support is one of the most used terms in business, but in reality the least exercised. Over the years there have been hundreds of examples of football teams that had an amazing offense, or an amazing defense, yet was still unsuccessful. This illustrates the lack of support on a team. No matter how charged a team is and how focused they maybe on their goal, without support they quickly start to lose focus and dissention amongst the ranks begins. I can't count the number of times I have seen a highly motivated, well organized team that would get derailed due to lack of support. It never ceases to amaze me how frequently in business a team will be given a task, and not the proper tools, equipment, information, etc., to be successful. Going back to football analogies, how successful would a football team be, if they were sent out on the field with no equipment? No helmets, shoulder pads, cleats, etc... it wouldn't matter how talented they were, how organized, or how clear the vision was that's provided; they literally could not be successful.

A team's ability to be successful will greatly depend on the support they receive from the top down. It may be equipment, tools, information, or just emotional support. The key is that all teams need support and you need to be diligent in providing them that support. Support usually starts to break down as the team starts to acquire small successes. The average manager will feel like "they've got this" and leave them alone. When the team asks for help, he will jump in, but otherwise leaves them to do what they do. As more time passes the average manager will have new projects on their plate and even when the team needs help, the manager will figure "the team can figure that out without my help." Once again to use the football analogy, imagine if a head coach just stopped coaching, or practicing because their team won a game? Would the team continue to win every game? Probably not.

So with all this in mind, how do you avoid the pitfalls of the average manager? Simply; become a coach. Understand that to manage a successful team you need to lend ongoing support, even when the team is doing a great job. Let them know they are doing a great job. Remind them of the common goal and their sense of purpose. Finally, always let them know how valuable they are, and their role in the successful outcome of the project.

It is easy to manage and stay on top of a poorly performing team. You know there is a problem and it demands your attention. Usually the problems stem from one of the included principles you will learn. If you are missing any of these principles the team has an increased chance of failure. We will cover in more detail the specific principles and how to apply them later.

Comradery is a strong part of what drives a team. While not everyone will always get along with each other, as a whole they have to believe in each other and honestly know that each member of the team has something to offer and is willing to work as hard as the rest of the team. This is where many teams fall apart. It seems that in every office I have been brought into, there is someone who doesn't carry their weight, or is harmful to the team. I implore you; if you want to be successful get rid of that person immediately. People like this are a cancer to a high performing team. People will ask the question, "Why should I work so hard if, he doesn't have to?" Also the issue of reward comes into play. A team's reward should be equal to all members. For example, in football just because the touchdown scoring play was more spectacular, it is still only worth six points. So with that idea, the members of the team that are working hard are earning rewards for the slackers of the team. This is a sure way to bring on dysfunction amongst your team. To build true team comradery you need trust. If the team can't trust someone, you have increased your chances of failure.

Competition. While there are many schools of thought on this, I truly believe that competition brings out the best in people and product. Whether people want to admit it or not, everyone wants to be considered a superstar in their profession. Without competition a team has little motivation. The competition doesn't have to be with each other, it may be to outperform last year's budget, or design a product with fewer resources, or just simply crush your local competition. No matter what drives the competition you should make it clear to the team, who or what their competition is. This is part of knowing what the common goal is and how we will know if we are on track.

Success. Success drives us all. Anyone who tells you that they don't care about success is more than likely lying to you and/or themselves. If success didn't drive people, then there would be no need for large luxury cars, homes, and boats. People are always trying to keep up with the Jones'. While I don't subscribe to that kind of thinking, I do admit that I feel good when I hit my mark, get through to a client, or help turn around a company that asked for my help. Success is what lets us all know it was worth it. Success is what validates our opinion of ourselves and success-or at least the hope of success-is what drives a team. As Vince Lombardi said, "If winning isn't important, why do we keep score?"

Chapter 4

What Makes A High Performing Team?

In my experience I have found that five things

create a high performing team:

☐ Vision

☐ Practice

☐ Clear Roles

☐ Accountability

☐ Rewards

While this parallels a lot of what we have

covered already I felt it was important enough to capture

in this section. The difference is between a team and a

high performing team. No team can become a high

performing team without these five principles. So let's

quickly cover them as they apply to this section.

Vision is what the coach's idea of the completed effort will be. In Football this would be standing on the podium holding up the Lombardi Trophy at the end of the year. The vision has to include all the principles learned thus far but it is imperative to have the entire team picture what the final outcome will be. The entire team needs to feel what it will be like to stand on that platform and hoist that trophy. This plays into trust, support, purpose, comradery, etc. A well defined vision will clearly layout the expectations of the team and will solidify their ability to focus on the primary objective. A coach's ability to have his team see, feel, taste, and smell, his vision is truly what separates the good from the great. Simply put, a team without vision is blind.

Practice. How can anyone become great without practice? Can you imagine someone who has never played a piano, sitting in front of one and instantly being able to play Mozart's Franz Liszt Hungarian Rhapsody No. 2? Not likely. So, any team needs to practice or train for success. Again, this is rarely done in the corporate world. You are just expected to know what to do and how to perform at a high level. I believe that truly successful companies understand that training and education is the only path to building a high performing team. The idea that you can hire great people is rarely true. While it does happen from time to time, in most cases great talent is bread from within.

So staying along the football theme, how successful would a team be, no matter how talented, if they never practiced? The part that people never see are the hours, weeks, and months that a team trains before walking onto the field. This is the same in business.

Training and education play a big role in the success of a team. So make sure that the proper practice is part of your support structure.

Clearly Defined Roles. As I stated before, every team member needs to know their role in the team dynamic. While everybody wants to be the Quarterback, the truth of the matter is, the quarterback would be useless without the offensive line to block for him, the receivers to run routes and catch his throws, or the backs to carry the ball and push the pile forward. Also, as we discussed, without a good defense, your offense has no chance of winning the game. In order for a team to be effective and build trust, they need to know who will be doing what job, and that they possess the skills to successfully complete that job. In many cases I have found that there is no structure in an office or team and hardly ever clearly defined roles. This is a major step in the right direction if your company or team falls into this mold. Take the time to evaluate each team member, analyze what their strengths are and put them in the best position to succeed. Once every team member knows what their role and responsibilities are, they will surprise you with their performance.

Accountability is undoubtedly the main ingredient missing in most of corporate America. The one common thread I seem to find, the deeper I dig into large companies, is the blame game. It seems that higher level executives got to where they are by passing the buck down the ladder. Whatever takes the focus off of them right? Wrong! How can you build trust without integrity?

I recently read a great story about a CEO that was planning on stepping down and wanted to name a new heir to the throne. He gave each candidate a pot with dirt in it; he told them that each pot held a seed. They were responsible for the care of the seed, and in one year he would name the next CEO based on how successfully they nurtured their seeds, they needed to water them, and fertilize them, and bring back whatever grew.

All of the candidates were very excited about their chances. About two weeks later they were all in a meeting and some of the candidates were talking about how their seeds were starting to grow into little seedlings. One of the candidates became concerned because his had not shown any sign of life yet. He had been carefully watering it, and talking to it, and making sure it got a little sun each day, but nothing was growing yet.

A few weeks later, some of the candidates were excitedly talking about how much their seeds had grown, and how they were becoming little plants now. But the same candidate who had worked so hard still had nothing happening in his pot; he told his wife he was concerned. She told him to just keep caring for it, and it was bound to grow.

At the summer picnic, about 6 months since he was given his seed, he overheard 3 of the candidates talking about how their plants had grown into little trees already, and how strong and healthy they were. His heart was beating really fast, and he felt a little sick with worry, he couldn't stop thinking that he wasn't just going to lose the CEO position, but he was going to be fired. He did his best to remain calm, and just kept on feeding and watering his pot of dirt, and hoped that somehow, it would grow.

When the day finally arrived to bring their seeds back to the CEO and show him what they had grown, everyone was smiling as they brought in the most beautiful trees he had ever seen. One was a flowering tree covered in pink flowers, another had lovely white blossoms, some had fruit, and it was amazing to see how well they had done.

All except for the one candidate who just never could get anything to grow. He was horror stricken; he kept his eyes down and shrunk low in his seat, hoping no one would notice. When the CEO got to him, he sort of stopped and stared at the dirt in the pot. "What happened here?" he asked. Swallowing hard, the candidate explained all of the things he had done to try to nurture the seed, how he had watered it, and fertilized it, given it plenty of sun, and he just didn't know why it wouldn't grow, he apologized for his failure, and was ready to leave, weighed down by the disappointment he must have caused his boss.

Then the CEO surprised him by saying, "Everyone, please look at this pot, all of you have done some amazing things with your seeds, but here, this pot is still just dirt with nothing growing in it." They all came to look and gave the poor candidate disapproving looks.

Then the CEO looked intently at the suffering candidate and announced, "You are our new CEO!"

Stunned, the new CEO asked. "How is that possible when my seed never grew? I failed."

The retiring CEO said, "No, you were the only honest candidate here, the seeds I gave to everyone were dead, and they could not have grown, so by coming here with just a pot of dirt, you have shown your integrity. Even though you believed you failed, you came here, and showed me your pot; you are the only one who deserves to be the CEO of this company."

No successful team can be built without Trust, and Accountability is a key component of Trust. Every team member needs to know their role and all team members need to know the results of their efforts. Just like a football team knows when the quarterback throws an interception or a back fumbles the ball. That is when the team comes together and picks up the ball, or firms up the defense. In business, these same rules apply. Every team member needs to be accountable for their mistakes as well as their successes. Once everyone knows where they stand as a team, then they can perform as a team. However, in many cases I have seen things hidden from other team members in an attempt to "Keep the Peace". If anyone really believes that there are secrets in corporate America, or even in a small company, then you should get your head out of the sand and look around. Be honest and up front with your team and hold them accountable for their performance.

Rewards. As we have already discussed, a football team wouldn't have much success if no one kept score. In football the rewards are the points on the board and a mark in the win column at the end of the game. Oh, if it were only that simple in business. Every time I walk into a new division or company I ask the same question, "How do you know if you are doing a good job?" It never ceases to amaze me that over and over again I get the same answer, which is silence. I then say, "Let me rephrase that, does your boss think you're doing a good job?" Again no answer or, "I would hope so." What does that tell you? No one really knows if they are doing a good job! If you have clear accountability and clear rewards, then everyone knows if they are doing well or not. If they continue to gain rewards (in football=points) then they know they are doing well and will get slaps on the back from their teammates for their outstanding performance. If they are doing poorly (in football= fumbling the ball) then they are supported by the team and brought up to a higher level. In this simple example you can begin to understand how important little rewards can be for the success of a team. Too often managers want to use negative re-enforcement to try and get results. I have always felt that you get better results when you –As Ken Blanchard would say- "Catch them doing something right". These rewards do not need to be monetary, or expensive. In some cases it is as simple as peer recognition. You have to decide what will fit in your company's structure and budget. I have heard of ideas ranging from a special chair at the meeting table for the best performer of the week, to an all expense paid trip to Hawaii for four. It really depends on the risk, and your imagination. Once you put all these structural keys in place you have the right environment for a high performing team.

Chapter 5

Why Can't I Just Put Talented People in the Right Position and Be Successful?

Too many times it has been tried in sports with no success. An eager owner, with too much money, buys the best talent available and puts them all on the same team. They never become a championship team. So the natural question is why? Simple, the Coach. You can have the most dynamic, talented team in the world but without structure and strong leadership they will ultimately fail. In most cases when a team of over achievers is put together, there are a lot of egos that come along with the talent. This requires an even stronger core structure and clear plan. If you take these people and put them together without strong leadership and structure, they will eat each other alive. Don't get me wrong, if you can get a superstar on your team, you should always accept them. However, be sure that you are a strong enough leader to keep the team focused and not let distractions interfere with the primary objective. In many cases you can take an enthusiastic, less skilled group of people and turn them into a high performing team by giving them a clear vision and the proper support they require. This will time and time again, produce successful results. It will also have the added benefit of building your next level of leaders. As previously noted, rarely do you hire someone great; you build them through training and support.

Chapter 6

Why a Coach?

The Coach

I tell everyone to be a coach not a boss. The reason is that a boss only cares about the bottom line and growth of the company. I realize that this is not always the case and there are many great bosses out there. However, I would argue that the bosses that are deemed as great would fall more into a coaches profile than a boss. A coach wants to win, no question about that. But he also cares about the health of the team, the satisfaction of his supporting coaches, each individual player's career, etc, etc, etc. A coach leaves it all on the field. His team knows his trials, his successes, and his personal goals. A coach brings the best out of their players and the assistant coaching staff, and they, in turn, bring out the best in the coach. A good coach takes all the blame and none of the credit.

The one thing that really differentiates a great coach from the standard boss or manager is that a coach trains and practices with his players to make them the best. The coach knows that someday his assistant coaches and players will be coaches of a different team, or maybe replace him? That never stops a coach from teaching and training the team. Can you picture how successful a team would be if a coach didn't give away his best plays, for fear that someone may steal them? This happens every day in the business world. Small minded managers and bosses honestly believe they are providing themselves with job security by keeping everyone down. I have always felt that you should be training your replacement all the time, and that everybody from the mailroom to the boardroom should feel like they have the opportunity to move all the way up the company ladder and sit in the CEO's chair. It makes me sick when I see weak people that are usually the cancer we discussed earlier, hide things from people so they will be the only ones who know how to do certain things in the company. In my world that is your quickest way to unemployment.

A coach will also get in the trenches with the team. He will be out in the rain, the cold, the heat, the wind, whatever Mother Nature throws at them, practicing, coaching, hitting, running. This lets the team know the coach is a team member. He doesn't just sit in an air-conditioned office telling everyone what they are doing wrong.

In many cases I will ask Manager's, "How often do you get out on the floor, or in the field and talk with your team?" The answers I get are always what I would want to hear, but when the same question is asked of the team members, they tell a different story all together. You need to be out in the elements of production. You need to smell what your team smells, feel what your team feels, and most importantly, listen to what your team says.

Chapter 7

Making Sure You Have the Right Talent

A coach's number one job is analyzing the talent. He needs to know who does what the best, and put them in the best position to succeed. Some coaches are better at this than others and that is why you will see varying levels of success throughout an organization.

There is an old saying "that dog won't hunt." While funny, it is true. Some people just aren't proficient at some things. As an example, take Tom Brady, arguably the best QB to ever play football. However, put him on a professional basketball team, and he is unlikely to be a superstar, let alone score a single basket. The term 'fish out of water' comes to mind when I am faced with this scenario. In business this happens frequently.

People who have financial backgrounds are put into management positions, people with strong management skills are put into financial positions, and so on. A good coach has to understand the talent and know what their limitations are in the overall organization. Ultimately it is the coach's responsibility to make sure that they have assembled the right team and put the right people in the right positions for success.

Sometimes it is hard for mangers to get the right people in the right positions, because the team members are afraid to say, "I am not good at that", or "I have never done that before." That comes back to the environment and culture of your company. Team members need to feel comfortable to say, "I am willing to try that but that is not one of my strengths." Once that culture exists, then you can easily find who fits what role in the team dynamic.

Chapter 8

Talent and Attitude

Another important key to having the right talent is effort and attitude. As I touched on earlier, the effort and attitude needs to be congruent throughout the team. A single slacker in the team will bring down the entire empire. No one team member should ever be lacking in their overall effort. We have all heard the term in sports; give it 110%. While mistakes will happen, and balls will be fumbled, the effort needs to always be 110%. The right attitude will take care of the mistakes as long as the team's effort is always focused and steadfast.

The attitude of the team needs to be one of support. In Football when a QB throws and interception, you don't see the team ostracize him, usually they are all patting him on the back and saying, "We'll get them next time." The defense goes out on the field and does their best to get the ball back into the QBs hands. The coach goes over to discuss what went wrong, the OC (Offensive Coach) sends down pictures of the formations so he will know what to look for next time. In short, the team comes together to lend support and learn from their mistakes. When the time comes back around for the QB to hit the field, they are better prepared for success on this effort. There is no question that the QB will get the ball again, and be given a chance at redemption.

The same holds true for business. When mistakes happen, and they will, the team needs to come together and help support and improve the whole team. There is no room for finger pointing or blame. They all win or lose as a team. That is the driving attitude of a winning team.

Chapter 9

Ethics

The final piece to having the right team is a unified sense of ethics. While this includes the right attitude, it goes deeper than that. An attitude can be adjusted, learned, or enforced. Ethics are something deeply ingrained in a person's soul. If someone has certain traits, selfishness, dishonesty, carelessness, etc... the chances of them ever changing are limited. You want to make sure that everyone on your team has the same core sense of ethics. This goes from the top down. Everyone involved with the team needs to know that they are dealing with a model of integrity. They all have to believe that they will not get thrown under a bus as soon as things start to go sideways. In short they need to know that the coach has their back. A team needs to know that their coach is a person of integrity and they can trust the coach even when things get rough. It is a question of character and commitment. If a team senses for one second that the coach has lost his commitment, or if they question the coach's character, all is lost and the chances for success are gone.

A final note to having the right talent. In order to achieve success you must be a true leader. Even with the best team and all the other principles learned within this teaching, you cannot succeed without true leadership. A coach is the leader. All successes and failures start and finish with the coach. It is only when things go bad, that your character and commitment will ever be tested. And it is only once you have been tested that you can reveal your true leadership. Anyone can be a good leader when things are going well and success is on the rise. The true test of a leader is will they still stand at the head of the

ship through the storm?

Chapter 10

Providing the Right Equipment

As I covered previously under support, how successful would a football team be, if they were sent out onto the field with no helmets, shoulder pads, cleats, etc...? The chances for any level of success would be highly improbable. This is mirrored in business. People are put into positions with certain expectations, and then not given the equipment to succeed. Let me clarify that when I say equipment or tools this refers to any need of the team. In many cases this is the proper training. However, I have also seen neglect in equipment and information. To have a successful team you have to provide them with the proper equipment to perform their task. Like the old saying, "I'll score you a touchdown coach, but you have to throw me the ball."

Whether it is training, computers, mobile devices, information, or executive support, to be a good coach you have to give the players the tools to excel. Without that key element you are setting them up for failure. Throughout the years I have seen many managers that hold back giving their team the tools they need to succeed. While I would always get multiple excuses, it always came down to money. I can't even begin to tell you how many times I have heard that excuse and it turned out that it was costing more money to avoid the proper tools than to provide the team with the needed equipment.

I have always subscribed to the school of thought that if there is a tool that increases the efficiency of a team member, you shouldn't even think about it, just get it. In most every business model the variable expense is labor. If a class for a few hundred dollars will increase their productivity, then get them the training! If a Smartphone will increase their efficiency, then get it! Almost every time you run this scenario you will find the benefits outweigh the costs. It will also show your level of commitment to your team to get them the best and most current tools for success. Bottom-line, don't send your team out on the field without helmets, they are just going to get hurt and you will not be successful.

Chapter 11

Developing the Right Game Plan

It is the coach's responsibility to develop the right game plan. If the coach put together the right game plan, and follows all the other principles that he's laid out, then there is a great chance for success. However, if the coach puts together a bad game plan, regardless of everything else, the team will fail.

In football a coach watches hours and hours of tape, gets second opinions, practices scenarios, and does about 100 other things each week just to come up with the game plan for that week's game. Can you imagine if every manager put that much energy into every project? The results would be staggering.

As a coach you need to develop the right game plan for each project. Every angle needs to be covered and thought through. You should run scenarios through your head and develop contingency plans. All great coaches have a plan B, C, D, etc...

In business, the right game plan will have all of the details covered. At a minimum you should develop;

☐ An org. chart with each team member's position

☐ Clearly defined roles for each team member

☐ An escalation chart

☐ A flow chart showing the processes involved

☐ Benchmarks for performance

☐ Goals & timeframes

☐ Contingency Plans

☐ Performance metrics

☐ Reward Program (what does the team get in return)

A proper game plan in business will require a solid structure as noted above and furthermore, as a coach, you will want to include as much information as possible to insure the success of your team. So whenever applicable the coach should prepare the following information for the team:

☐ Historical internal performance metrics, financial models, lessons learned, etc...

☐ Historical external performance metrics, financial models, lessons learned, etc...

The more information you can gather based on past efforts, the more it will help the team learn from others mistakes, rather than repeating them. Just like a coach watches game film, you should study the historical data involved with other similar efforts. The more due diligence you do on the front end of a project the better your chances for success.

Unfortunately many managers don't give this level of support during the start up period of a project. More often than not, a team is thrown together, based on availability rather than proficiency and little to no effort is given to the team dynamic or structure. One of the best things you can do as a coach is to set up your team for success before you even start the project. You will increase the chances of success and your team will know your level of commitment. The standard rule of thumb is that if little effort is put on the front end, even less effort will be required on the back end, kind of like biking up a hill, and coasting down the other side.

Chapter 12

Common Goal

In previous pages I have talked about the common goal and how that translates to football. In business, a team knowing the common goal is crucial to their success. However, the fact is that in business a common goal is not so common. How can you really expect a team to be successful if they do not know the main objective or goal? Imagine, in the football analogy, a team that doesn't know the point of the game is to cross the goal line. How successful would they be?

In business you need to make sure that your team understands the common goal. The entire team needs to know the game plan, how to win and how to lose. You need to make sure that prior to starting a project you gather the team and let them know why they were chosen, what will be expected, and when. Furthermore, they need to understand how they will be measured and how they will be rewarded. This will bring everyone together on what the game plan and common goals are for the team and what needs to happen to achieve success.

A team needs to know how they are progressing towards the goal. This, in many companies, eludes the team. I have not been able to determine if that is by chance or design, but in most cases it seems to be by design. I have been told by some, they are afraid to let the team know if they are doing a great job, for fear they will demand more money, lose focus, or get complacent. Really, how would they feel if they were kept in the dark? Imagine the president of a company that didn't share the financial reports with the shareholders. How well would that go over?

You need to share all the information with your team, both good and bad. Only then can trust be developed. The main ingredient in a team is trust. How can you expect a team to function if you can't trust them with financial and performance information? Do you really expect a team to trust you if you don't trust them? It will never happen. You get what you give in this world and it is no different in business.

Just to complete this thought I am going to stray from the football analogy for one second. I love to play golf. However, I am not very good since I don't have a lot of time to practice. I do try and get to the driving range whenever I can to at least hit a bucket of balls. Yesterday, I was hitting some balls and reflecting on this section and I realized how golf could apply to this section as well. Not sharing information with your team is like golfing without a ball, or even worse, like golfing with a blindfold. As I stood there with my eyes closed, I swung at the ball and hit it. I knew I hit it due to the sound it made. It sounded like I hit it really well. However, how would I know what really happened until I opened my eyes? Alas, I shanked it right along with most of my other shots. But for a second, I thought I hit a great ball. Maybe I should always keep my eyes closed!

This is what you are doing to your team when you do not share information. They may think they are crushing the ball, when in reality they are shanking it. On the other hand, they may be crushing it when they think they shanked it. Take of your team's blindfolds off and let them see how they are doing, and you will begin

to see the results almost immediately.

Chapter 13

Measurable Success

So far I have referred to accountability,
performance metrics, rewards, penalties, etc... These are
all things that, as explained, are a major ingredient to the
success of a team. So bringing together the Football
Management theme, this applies to both equally. In
business, like football, you need to have measurable
performance metrics. These can be motivational,
financial, numerical; it all depends on your business
model and discipline. Just like a football team has first
downs, in business you need to have recognizable small
victories as part of your project plan. This will let
everyone know they are on track to achieving the goal.

This will also let them know if they are losing
yardage by not meeting these small victories on the

expected timeline, or within the expected budgets. Just like penalties in football, your team may experience small set- backs. Adjustments need to be made to gain back the lost yardage, (in business time or money), then aim for the next small victory or first down. This is the best way to keep a team focused. In football or business, these first downs or small victories, get the team a whole new set of downs to try and go another ten yards. Slowly moving down field to the main objective, crossing the goal line.

In the end the team will have been focused on all the small victories (First downs), and before they know it they are crossing the goal line and scoring a touchdown! In some cases they may have to settle for results that were profitable but not what they had planned for, this would be a field goal in football. You still had some success, but not a touchdown. That needs to be

celebrated as well. Then go back and analyze what kept

it from being a touchdown, and try again.

Chapter 14

Sideline Coaching and Adjustments

This section may be the part that finally makes
you start to understand how football applies to
management. Sideline coaching is what we as managers
do every day. We have teams out there working for us
and as information comes in we analyze, adjust, and re-
engage.

In football, as a team first takes the field, they
start with the game plan as practiced all week. Whether
it is offense or defense doesn't really matter, but let's use
offense for this example. Almost always the coach has a
script for the first three plays. The QB, in business this
would be the project manager, reads the defense and
adjusts based on how the defense is set up. They run the

plays as practiced with varying results, all the time the coaches are on the sidelines discussing and learning what works and doesn't work based on that challenge. If the team was unsuccessful in achieving the first down, they come off the field.

Once the offense is off the field the work begins. The entire coaching staff starts to analyze the formations based on pictures taken from the booth. The QB sits with the receivers and discusses why the routes were not working, the whole team is on the sidelines making adjustments, analyzing and preparing for their next effort. They are behind the scheduled effort and need to get back in the game. The funny part is that all this happens even when they are successful. The idea being, we can always do better.

In business, the same applies. When a team first starts the project, they perform based on the game plan set forth by the coach or manager. The Project Manager may make some minor adjustments based on what he experiences during the first week, month, or whatever structure is set. This is where a high performing manager makes a difference. You need to check in on your team and see how they are progressing on the project. You need to lend support on making adjustments and analyzing what has happened thus far. You need to feed them with information on any recordable results to date. They may need different information, tools, equipment. Either way, if you are not part of the ongoing effort, then it will be difficult for you to lend the support needed. A good coach is always on the sidelines, coaching and supporting their team.

Given these two analogies, how successful would a team be if a head coach spent all week putting together the perfect game plan, however, there was no coaching staff on game day? Or, how about if after the team won the first game, the coach just stopped coaching? Even the best plans need adjustments. Things change and adjustments need to be made, so assuming that all will go as planned is a fool's game.

This seems to happen too often in business though. A dynamic team is put together and left to succeed or fail on their own. Or, in other cases a team is set up and monitored, but as soon as some success is achieved they are left alone, figuring that they've got it and will continue being successful.

Another type of sideline coaching applies to team member's attitudes. On any team egos and attitudes can arise. If left alone they can destroy a team. It is a coach's job to keep egos in check and squash any destructive attitudes before they have a chance to fester. Negativity is an issue that can quickly spread and destroy a team in a matter of days. So a coach needs to be on the sideline, always watching and ready to pounce on any destructive behavior.

Chapter 15

Penalties & Mistakes

In football and in business there needs to be penalties. A team needs to know the rules and what happens if they break them. Just like with a puppy or a child, if you set rules with no consequences, you will end up with a poorly trained dog or a misbehaved child. In business if you set rules with no consequences, you will have a team that breaks the rules. You need to set rules and penalties for breaking them. Just like in football they need to vary in levels of severity. There needs to be small reprimands to facilitate proper execution, and game changing penalties for major infractions. When it comes time to implement the penalty, make it quick, end with a positive such as, "You're better than this", and let it go. Do not continue to bring this up at later dates or degrade your team member. Most people want to do a good job and are not going to be happy they messed up. You yelling at them or constantly reminding them will only breed resentment.

Mistakes on the other hand, should not be reprimanded. Most mistakes are made due to a lack of training, lack of information, or lack of structure. I hate to tell you this, but those are your fault as a manager if they exist. It is your job to supply your team with the proper equipment, remember? So if a mistake happens it is usually your fault and not the fault of the team. However, there are some mistakes that are just a momentary lapse of judgment, and cannot be attributed to any one specific reason. In football this can be equated to the infamous Leon Lett play, where he ran the wrong way with the football. (Football fans will remember this bone head move) But just like fumbles, interceptions, and other unpleasant mistakes you should never come down on your team for things of this nature. You need to support them, let them know that nobody is perfect, and retrain them on how to avoid this mistake next time. The bottom line is that while there will be mistakes made, in the end you want to have a lot more 'at-a-boys' than 'uh-oh's'.

Chapter 16

Knowing the Final Score

So we have finally made it to the final section, knowing the final score. While everyone would like to win every game, it has only been done once, by my favorite team, the Miami Dolphins. The key to perfection is to always better yourself, even when things are great. I would venture to say that if you were to ask any of the team members of the '72 Dolphins, were you all perfect that season? Undoubtedly, they would say no! The key was at the end of every game they had more at-a-boys then uh-oh's. There were mistakes made in every game, on every down, but in the end they stayed focused and prevailed over their opponent.

Unlike the '72 Dolphins, most of us have to face failure. There will be projects that didn't get the planned results. It is in these failures that we will learn the most about our team and ourselves, for as I said before, your character cannot be revealed until it has been tested.

Whether you win or lose, you and your team need to know the final score. You should have documented proof of what transpired throughout this effort and what were the successes and failures. You need to analyze who performed well and who fell short. You should study the results and ask questions like what could we have done better, or is there something we were missing that could have increased our success? Once you have a complete debriefing of the events, take time to digest the information, and then make any necessary adjustments to personnel, equipment, training, etc...

Where this piece usually gets missed in when you win. In business if a project is successful, the team will usually be reassigned, or move on to another project. No thought is given to what made that project successful or how it could have been even more successful. You should always be striving to get better. Complacency is the death of any team on the field or in the office.

What truly separates the champions from the everyday teams is the pursuit for perfection. In order to be better than your competition you need to completely tear down the model for success into its most finite detail. Understand every step, every piece of information, why it worked, and is there room for improvement? Constantly striving to get better with every effort, a great team continues to learn and grow as long as they exist, never accepting success as a destination.

In the end it all comes down to the Coach and his team. Like in football, one is lost without the other and neither can succeed without the other's support. It is all for one and one for all. So get out there and start coaching your team to be the next world champions of business. And remember, that Team is actually an acronym, T.E.A.M. meaning:

Together Everyone Achieves More!

About the Author

Lucky Drake is a Director of Service and Critical Support, for the largest electrical and engineering firm in the world. Presently he oversees more than 150 employees worldwide. He works with some of the world's largest retailers, government agencies, and everything in between. Working his way up from the field as a Journeyman Electrician to a Master Electrician and then a Project Manager, to the executive position he holds now, he has learned many valuable lessons he shares in this manual.

Mr. Drake is a strong believer in teaching others, he has dedicated many hours to training team members, friends, and colleagues how to be successful and meet their personal goals. If he won the lottery, he says he would open a training center to teach anyone who is interested how to be successful and help those who need it, learn a trade to provide for their families.

Lucky Drake lives in Florida with his wife and three crazy Australian Shepherds. He has two children and one grandchild, so far. He enjoys spending time with family, fishing, and playing guitar in his free time.

You can find him on LinkedIn.

Also, check out his blog:

http://glenluckydrake.blogspot.com/